STRESS RELIEVING COLORING BOOK

COLOR THERAPY ACTIVITY BOOK FOR STRESS RELIEF

MY COLORING BOOK

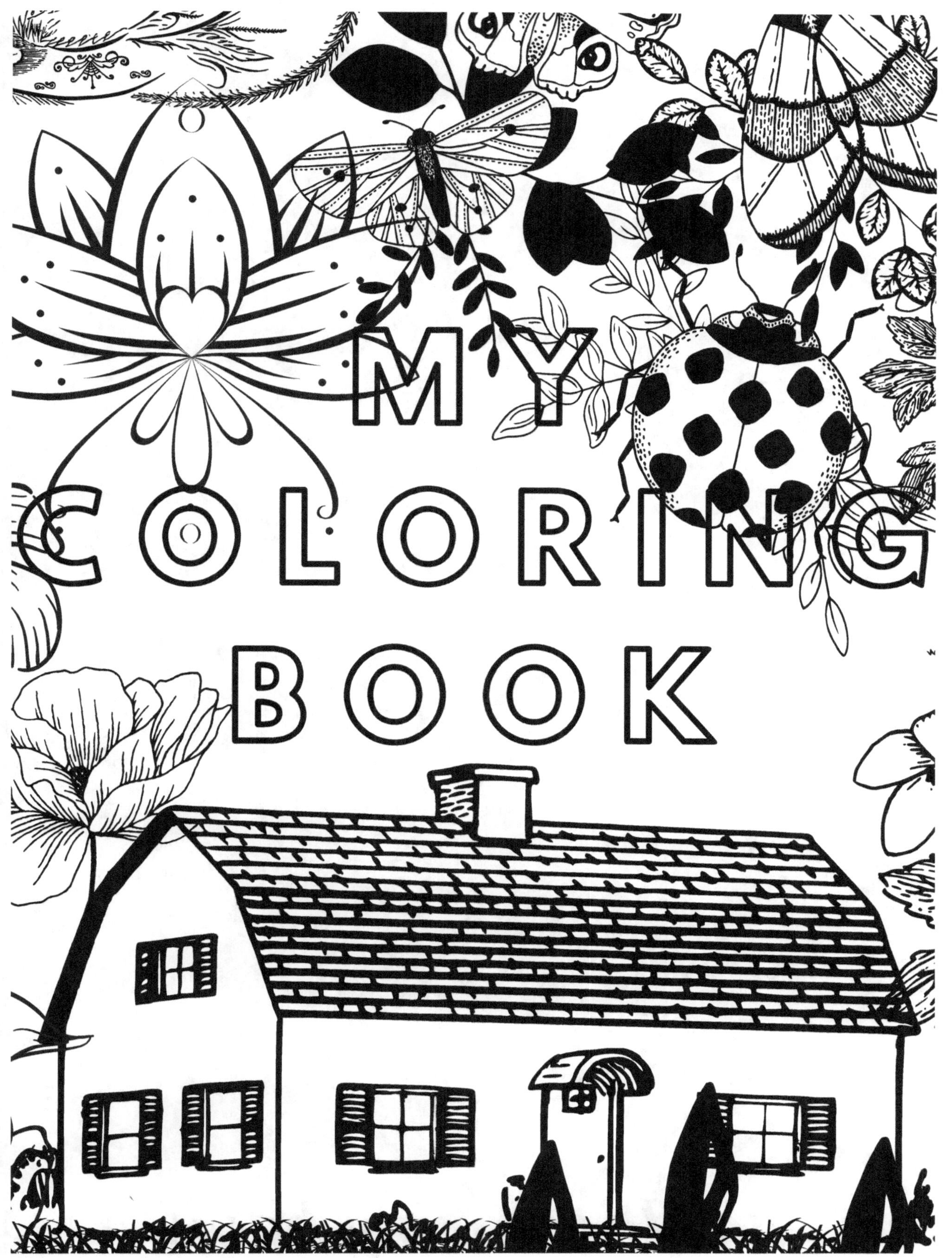
MY
COLORING
BOOK

adult coloring book

adult coloring book

adult coloring book

adult coloring book

adult coloring book

adult coloring book

adult coloring book

adult coloring book

adult coloring book

adult coloring book

adult coloring book

adult coloring book

adult coloring book

adult coloring book

adult coloring book

adult coloring book

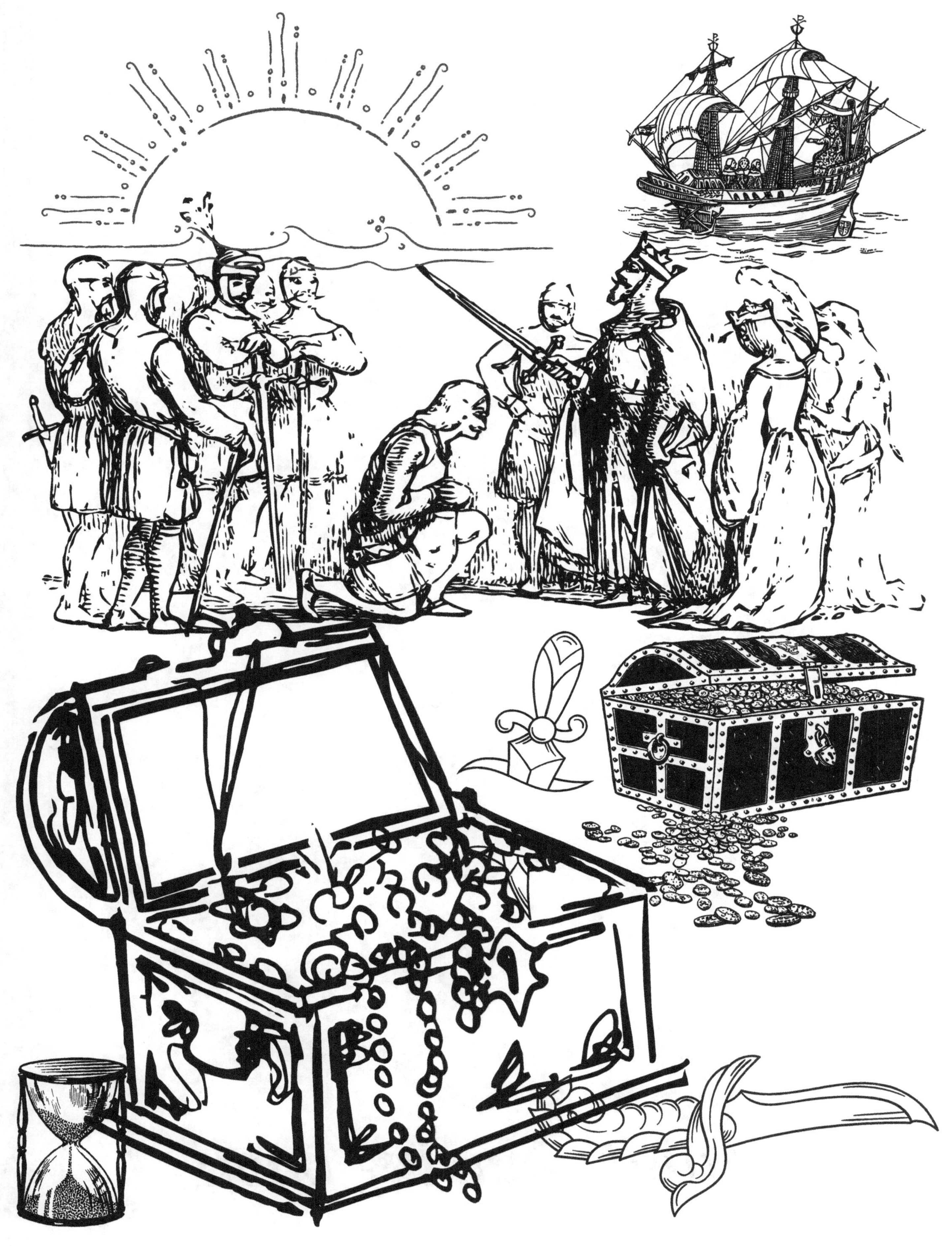

adult coloring book

adult coloring book

adult coloring book

adult coloring book

adult coloring book

adult coloring book

adult coloring book

adult coloring book

adult coloring book

adult coloring book